Epic Cars

Ferrari 812 Superfast

D1736825

JULIA GARSTECKI

BLACK
RABBIT
BOOKS

Bolt is published by Black Rabbit Books
P.O. Box 3263, Mankato, Minnesota, 56002.
www.blackrabbitbooks.com
Copyright © 2020 Black Rabbit Books

Marysa Storm, editor; Catherine Cates,
interior designer; Grant Gould, cover designer;
Omay Ayres, photo researcher

Library of Congress Cataloging-in-Publication Data
Names: Garstecki, Julia, author.
Title: Ferrari 812 Superfast / by Julia Garstecki.
Description: Mankato, Minnesota : Black Rabbit Books, [2020] | Series: Bolt.
Epic cars | Includes index. | Audience: Ages 9-12. | Audience: Grades 4 to 6.
Identifiers: LCCN 2018015957 (print) | LCCN 2018019364 (ebook) |
ISBN 9781680728446 (e-book) | ISBN 9781680728361 (library binding) |
ISBN 9781644660355 (paperback)
Subjects: LCSH: Ferrari 812 Superfast automobile–Juvenile literature.
Classification: LCC TL215.F47 (ebook) | LCC TL215.F47 G36 2020 (print) |
DDC 629.222/2-dc23
LC record available at https://lccn.loc.gov/2018015957

Special thanks to Justin Storm for his help with this book.

Printed in the United States. 1/19

Contents

CHAPTER 1

Racing

Down the Road

A Ferrari 812 Superfast rockets down the road. The supercar is hard to miss. The sun reflects off its body. It roars as it changes gears. The car speeds around curves with ease. Every move it makes looks effortless.

COMPARING METRIC HORSEPOWER

2018 Bugatti Chiron

2018 Ferrari 812 Superfast

2018 Lamborghini Aventador S

2018 McLaren 720S

metric horsepower

Fast and Powerful

Ferrari revealed the 812 Superfast in 2017. The supercar's name comes from its engine. The 12-**cylinder** engine produces 800 metric **horsepower**. It makes for one super fast, super powerful car.

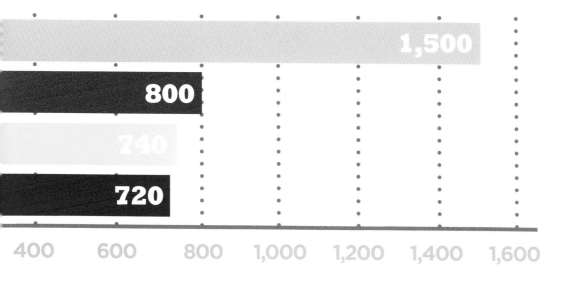

1,500

800

740

720

400 600 800 1,000 1,200 1,400 1,600

SPOILER

WHEELS

VENTS

LONG FRONT

GRILLE

CHAPTER 2

Design

Drivers love how the 812 looks.
It has a muscular, smooth design.
The front is long and sleek. It shares
several features, such as round
taillights, with classic Ferraris.

Ferrari released the 812 during the company's 70th anniversary.

Shaped for Speed

Many design features help the 812 drive at top speeds. The spoiler sits high. It creates **downforce**. Downforce makes the car stable at high speeds.

The front bumper
decreases drag
by pushing air
around the car.

13

Personalized

Buyers can personalize their 812s. The outside comes in 37 different colors. There are many interior colors to pick from too. Buyers can also choose seat shape and size. They can even pick the color of thread those seats are sewn with.

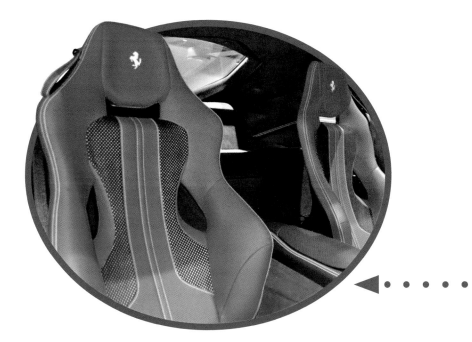

Three Seat Styles

DAYTONA
RACING SEATS

STANDARD
SEATS

CARBON FIBER
RACING SEATS

15

MANY CHOICES

Drivers have many options when buying their 812 Superfasts.

37
EXTERIOR
COLORS

15
INTERIOR
COLORS

9
CARPET COLORS

3
RIM STYLES

18
THREAD
COLORS

Incredible Interior

Inside, the 812 is stylish. Many features are circular. Designers wanted the dials to look like they floated. The car is small. But inside, it feels roomy and comfortable.

Loud on the Outside, Quiet on the Inside

Many car lovers enjoy the sound of a car's engine. They don't want to be overpowered by it while driving, though. The 812's interior has some soundproofing. The engine noises aren't as loud. Drivers can still enjoy its roar. But they aren't overwhelmed by it. Outside, people can hear the car long before they see it.

CHAPTER 3

Power and Performance

The 812 Superfast lives up to its name. It truly is super fast. It can reach 211 miles (340 kilometers) per hour. It takes only 2.9 seconds to hit 62 miles (100 km) per hour.

COMPARING TOP SPEEDS

2018 Aventador S

2018 McLaren 720S

2018 812 Superfast

2018 Porsche 911 GT3

miles per hour

217 (349 km)

212 (341 km)

211 (340 km)

198 (319 km)

160　170　180　190　200　210　220

The car's **suspension** helps keep the ride
smooth on bumpy roads.

Epic Steering

Fast cars need strong steering. The 812 has several systems that help it drive well. One system is Electric Power Steering (EPS). EPS works with the rest of the car. It helps the driver turn safely at high speeds. Other systems increase the car's **handling**. They improve response time. It's easier for drivers to manage the car's power.

By the Numbers

183.3 INCHES
(465.6 CM)
LENGTH

77.6 INCHES
(197.1 CENTIMETERS)
WIDTH

50.2
INCHES
(127.5 CM)
HEIGHT

VS·482524

2
TOTAL SEATING

ESTIMATED
HIGHWAY MILEAGE

about
16
miles (26 km)
per gallon

about
$308,000
base price

CHAPTER 4

An Epic Car

The 812 Superfast is one epic car.
It amazes drivers with its power and
beauty. It takes over the road and track.
There's no mistaking this
incredible car.

carbon fiber (KAR-buhn FAHY-bur)—a very strong, lightweight material

cylinder (SIL-en-dur)—a part of an engine

downforce (doun-FAWRS)—a force that increases the stability of a motor vehicle by pressing it downward

drag (DRAYG)—something that makes action or progress slow or more difficult

grille (GRIL)—a mesh framework covering the opening at the front of a car

handling (HAND-ling)—the way a car, motorcycle, or other vehicle drives

horsepower (HORS-pow-uhr)—a unit used to measure the power of engines

mileage (MAHY-lij)—the average number of miles a vehicle will travel on a gallon of gasoline

spoiler (SPOI-ler)—a device placed on a vehicle to reduce lift and increase drag; it "spoils" airflow.

suspension (suh-SPEN-shuhn)—the system of springs that supports the upper part of a vehicle on the axles

BOOKS

Cockerham, Paul W. *Ferrari: Pure Passion and Power*. Speed Rules! Inside the World's Hottest Cars. Broomall, PA: Mason Crest, 2018.

Fishman, Jon M. *Cool Sports Cars*. Awesome Rides. Minneapolis: Lerner Publications, 2019.

Kingston, Seth. *The History of Ferraris*. Under the Hood. New York: PowerKids Press, 2019.

WEBSITES

812 Superfast: Shift to the 12th Dimension
812superfast.ferrari.com/us/start

Build Your Own 812 Superfast
car-configurator.ferrari.com/812superfast

Ferrari 812 Superfast
www.caranddriver.com/ferrari/812-superfast

INDEX